T0199205

Rise and Shine
Fire Child

Veronica Red

Illustrated by Raquel Rodriguez

The morning has finally come.

Today will be bringing so much wonder and fun!

Later, I will be on a fabulous stage, happily singing and dancing,

Merrily flowing around with courage, feeling my spirit enhancing.

There has always been a knowing I would perform on a stage,

Enjoying the freedom and openness rather than feeling enclosed in a cage,

Showing the world what I have proudly learned and so truly love.

Achieving success and recognition will fit me like a glove.

Expressing my freedom through dance, fine-tuning my technique,

Following the beats of the music, activating the magic within.

Like a key unlocking my very own original blueprint,

Opening up to the richness of being proud and unique.

In time of practice, my audience has been my friends of the garden.

My sharp moves, twirls, and quick spins have left them feeling guarded.

Forgiving my friends for the confusion, watching them depart,

Smiling to reassure them, coaxing them back to my passionate, loving heart.

It's my masterpiece, my very own art.

Now is a time to expand, play with others, and be observed.

To blend and join in with all, my gifts will be seen and heard.

Untangling from limited beliefs and moving ahead,

Stepping out now, I'm ready and well prepared.

Through a tiny spark, I feel my energy begin to powerfully erupt;

My performing glow is shining and filtering out.

The crowd is cheering and celebrating the event.

So wonderful watching all enjoying the show, just like I have always dreamt.

Celebrations beaming from the stage to crowd and back again,

It's a fabulous way for the show to reach the end.

The applause is loud and colorful, exactly how I feel.

So refreshing to reveal all that was within concealed.

I always wondered what it would be like to be onstage.

I knew I could do it; it felt so natural for me to engage.

Time to rest and sit with my victory,

Intact and safe from any injury.

Reflecting and looking out my window, drawn to the rays of the sun,

With a smile I remember the sun is a star that shines on its own.

Copyright © 2018 by Veronica Red. 780367

ISBN: Softcover   978-1-9845-0433-3
       EBook   978-1-9845-0432-6

All rights reserved. No part of this book may
be reproduced or transmitted in any form or by
any means, electronic or mechanical, including
photocopying, recording, or by any information storage
and retrieval system, without permission in writing from
the copyright owner.

Print information available on the last page

Rev. date: 11/26/2018

To order additional copies of this book, contact:
Xlibris
1-800-455-039
www.xlibris.com.au
Orders@Xlibris.com.au

Printed in the United States
By Bookmasters